MiNi MaKeRs

mini
HOLIDAY
CRAFTS

by Rebecca Felix

Lerner Publications / Minneapolis

Lerner Publications Company
A division of Lerner Publishing Group, Inc.
241 First Avenue North
Minneapolis, MN 55401 USA

For reading levels and more information, look up this title at www.lernerbooks.com.

Main body text set in Bembo STD 16/25.
Typeface provided by Monotype Typography.

Library of Congress Cataloging-in-Publication Data

Names: Felix, Rebecca, 1984- author.
Title: Mini holiday crafts / by Rebecca Felix.
Description: Minneapolis : Lerner Publications, [2016] | Series: Mini makers | Audience: Ages 7-11. | Audience: Grades 4 to 6. | Includes bibliographical references and index.
Identifiers: LCCN 2016018571 (print) | LCCN 2016020015 (ebook) | ISBN 9781512426335 (lb : alk. paper) | ISBN 9781512428117 (eb pdf)
Subjects: LCSH: Handicraft–Juvenile literature. | Miniature craft–Juvenile literature. | Holiday decorations–Juvenile literature.
Classification: LCC TT900.H6 F45 2016 (print) | LCC TT900.H6 (ebook) | DDC 745.5–dc23

LC record available at https://lccn.loc.gov/2016018571

Manufactured in the United States of America
1-41384-23325-8/4/2016

Photo Acknowledgements
The images in this book are used with the permission of: © Mighty Media, Inc., pp. 4, 5, (bottom), 8 (left), 8 (right), 9 (top), 10, 11 (top), 11 (middle), 11 (bottom), 12, 13 (top), 13 (middle), 13 (bottom), 14, 15 (top), 15 (middle), 15 (bottom), 16, 17 (top), 17 (middle), 17 (bottom), 18, 19 (top), 19 (middle), 19 (bottom), 20, 21 (top), 21 (middle), 21 (bottom), 22, 23 (top), 23 (middle), 23 (bottom), 24, 25 (top), 25 (middle), 25 (bottom), 26, 27 (top), 27 (middle), 27 (bottom), 28 (top), 28 (middle), 28 (bottom), 29; © Aleksander Erin/Shutterstock Images, pp. 4 (paint and paintbrushes), 11 (paint and paintbrushes); © Monkey Business Images/Shutterstock Images, p. 5 (top); © Svitlana-ua/Shutterstock Images, pp. 5 (scissors and paper), 24 (scissors and paper); © Anastasia_Panait/Shutterstock Images, pp. 6 (glitter), 20 (glitter); © Christopher Futcher/iStockphoto, p. 7; © mayakova/Shutterstock Images, pp. 8 (sprinkles), 18 (sprinkles); © Kaesler Media/Shutterstock Images, p. 8 (party blower); © Buravchikova/Shutterstock Images, p. 9 (colored pencils); © Oksana Shufrych/Shutterstock Images, p. 9 (colored beads); © Coprid/Shutterstock Images, p. 9 (scissors); © mikeledray/Shutterstock Images, p. 9 (googly eyes); © Flower Studio/Shutterstock Images, p. 14 (green beads); © HamsterMan/Shutterstock Images, p. 16 (star confetti); © STILLFX/Shutterstock Images, p. 19 (ribbon).

Front cover: © Mighty Media, Inc.

Back cover: © Mighty Media, Inc. (left, right); © kemalbas/iStockphoto (buttons); © Ryan Lindberg/iStockphoto (scissors).

CONTENTS

Getting Started
MINI HOLIDAY MAGIC

What if you could carry a little piece of holiday cheer with you everywhere you go? Imagine a birthday balloon no bigger than a button. Now picture a thimble-sized turkey. What about a holiday wreath the size of a ring, or sparkly fireworks no bigger than your hand?

Tiny things **fascinate** many people. Small objects are like little secrets. An itty-bitty item can be easily hidden. People need to get very close to **examine** tiny **trinkets**. The secret of small things is almost like magic. Create little bits of this magic all year long. Learn how to make mini crafts to help you celebrate the holidays in a big way!

Before You Begin
SLOW AND STEADY

Making mini crafts is tons of fun. But it can also be frustrating! Super-small supplies can be hard to pick up, hold steady, and assemble. It is easy to lose track of teeny buttons, beads, and other small supplies. Working with tiny crafts can be challenging. One big cut could ruin your **petite** project if you're not careful!

Before beginning your mini holiday crafts, gather your supplies. Many tiny craft materials can be found at a craft store. Or an adult can help you order supplies online. Make sure your work area is clear before you start crafting. This will help you keep an eye on tiny tools and itty-bitty parts. Good lighting makes it easier to clearly see your mini pieces and projects. Use small containers, bowls, and plates to keep track of small supplies. When you're ready to start crafting, work slowly! Taking your time will make completing your little creations easier and more fun!

Work Safely!

Some crafts require the use of sharp tools. That means they also require adult help. An adult will make sure your fingers, eyes, and workspace are protected as you craft amazing mini creations.

CELEBRATE
Creativity

Holidays are about celebrating! As you work on your mini holiday crafts, have fun and get creative. Think about fun extra features or cool designs you could add to your crafts. Maybe your mini wreath needs little berries made from beads. Would the itty-bitty piñata look **festive** covered in small **sequins**? Find out! Think of ways to make the crafts your own. Then try them out.

You can also get creative with the tools you use to assemble your tiny crafts. Think of small items that might make your work easier. Tweezers are the perfect tool for picking up teeny tiny beads. A toothpick can become a little paintbrush in a pinch. Create new uses for little tools. And find fun ways to add special touches to your mini holiday crafts.

TEENY TINY CLOVER PIN

Craft a lucky little clover pin to celebrate Saint Patrick's Day!

MATERIALS

- newspaper
- 4 sunflower seeds
- green and black paint
- paintbrushes
- pin and pin back
- clay
- strong, quick-setting glue
- scissors
- green floral wire

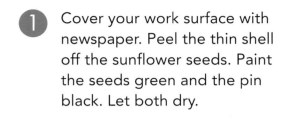

1. Cover your work surface with newspaper. Peel the thin shell off the sunflower seeds. Paint the seeds green and the pin black. Let both dry.

1

2. Stick the pin in the clay. Glue the painted seeds to the pin's flat surface. Arrange the seeds in a clover design.

3. Cut a short piece of floral wire. It should be 1 to 2 inches (2.5 to 5 centimeters) long. This will be the clover's stem. Bend one stem end to make a curve. Glue the straight end of the stem to the pin, between two seeds.

2

4. Let the glue on your pin dry overnight. Then sport your mini clover pin on Saint Patrick's Day or any time you need a little luck!

3

MINI KINARA

Celebrate Kwanzaa with a cute little **kinara**!

MATERIALS

- 8 small thimbles
- hammer
- newspaper
- red, green, and black paint
- paintbrushes
- all-purpose glue
- wooden craft stick
- 1 each red, green, black, and orange pipe cleaners
- pencil
- scissors
- 2 yellow pipe cleaners

3

4

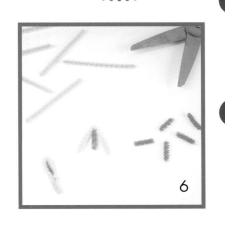

6

1. With an adult's help, hammer the thimble bottoms until they are flat. Then, cover your work surface with newspaper. Paint three thimbles red, three thimbles green, and two thimbles black. Let the paint dry.

2. Glue one black thimble open-end down in the center of the craft stick. Glue the other black thimble open-end up on top of the first thimble.

3. Glue the green thimbles open-end up to the stick on one side of the black thimbles. Repeat on the other side with the red thimbles.

4. Wrap the green pipe cleaner around a pencil. Remove, and cut small **coils**, each about ½ inch (1.3 cm) high. Place a coil inside each green thimble. Repeat with the black and red pipe cleaners to fill each black and red thimble.

5. Cut seven small pieces of the orange pipe cleaner. Each should be about as long as your fingernail. Next, cut seven pieces of the yellow pipe cleaners. Make each about three times as long as each orange piece.

6. Bend a yellow pipe cleaner piece in half. Then tuck an orange pipe cleaner piece inside the yellow piece to look like a candle flame. Twist the yellow ends together with the orange end to form a flame shape. Then stick the pipe cleaner ends into each of the pipe cleaner coils you made. Repeat until you've made flames for all the thimbles. Then set out this cute kinara to celebrate Kwanzaa!

WEE CHRISTMAS WREATH

This itty-bitty beaded wreath will brighten a small spot during the Christmas season!

MATERIALS

- green craft wire
- scissors
- ruler
- tape
- 2 shades small green beads
- small red beads
- key ring
- thin red ribbon
- all-purpose glue

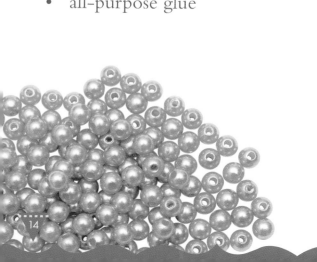

14

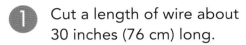

3

4

6

1. Cut a length of wire about 30 inches (76 cm) long.

2. Wrap a small piece of tape about 4 inches (10 cm) in from one wire end.

3. With the tape at the bottom, start stringing the green beads on the wire. Add a red bead every so often to look like a berry.

4. When the wire is covered in beads, wrap it around the key ring. Continue wrapping until the entire ring is covered.

5. Remove the tape from the end of the wire. Remove any extra beads, and twist the two wire ends together. Twist or tie the extra wire length in a loop to hang the wreath.

6. Tie the ribbon in a tiny bow. Glue it to your wreath. Now hang your wee wreath anywhere a little Christmas cheer is needed!

STRING OF TEENSY STARS OF DAVID

Make a shimmery **garland** to celebrate Hanukkah with some sparkle!

MATERIALS

- cardboard
- ruler
- pen
- scissors
- blue craft foam
- newspaper
- all-purpose glue
- silver glitter
- thread
- needle

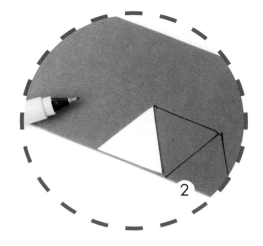

1. Measure and draw a triangle on the cardboard. Each side should be 1 inch (2.5 cm) long. Cut out the triangle.

2. Use the cardboard triangle to trace two triangles of craft foam. Repeat for each star you want on the garland. Cut out the triangles.

3. Cover your work surface with newspaper. Put a small puddle of glue on the newspaper. Dip two sides of each triangle in the glue. Then sprinkle glitter all over the glue-covered sides. Let the triangles dry. Repeat with the third side of each triangle.

4. Overlap two triangles so one triangle's point is on top and the other triangle's point is on the bottom. Glue together. Repeat with all of your triangles.

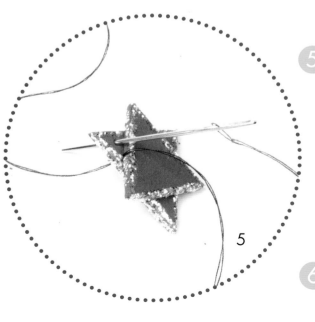

5. Cut a piece of thread twice as long as the garland will be. With an adult's help, thread the needle by poking the thread through the needle's hole. Then tie the thread ends together in a double knot. Poke the needle through the back of one star's tip. Then poke the needle back through the front of the tip, and pull the thread through. Repeat until all stars are on the thread.

6. Space the stars evenly on the thread. Then cut the thread near the needle and knot the two loose ends. Hang your shimmering garland at your next Hanukkah gathering!

SUPER-SMALL BIRTHDAY BALLOONS

Create a teeny balloon bouquet for a fun birthday surprise!

MATERIALS

- wire
- ruler
- scissors
- balloons
- small wooden beads
- ribbon

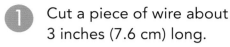

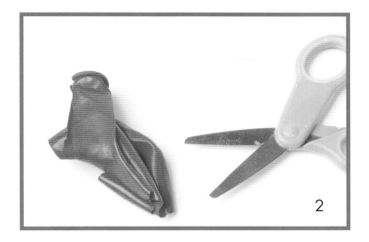

1. Cut a piece of wire about 3 inches (7.6 cm) long.

2. Cut a balloon open.

3. Wrap a bead in the balloon material. Then twist the balloon at the bottom of the bead.

2

4. Wrap the wire piece around the twisted part of the balloon to secure it.

5. Cut off any **excess** balloon.

6. Repeat steps 1 through 5 to make a bunch of bitty balloons! Tie them together using ribbon. Then surprise a favorite birthday boy or girl with a pint-sized balloon bouquet!

6

BITTY VALENTINE BOXES

Create little boxes stuffed with tiny treats and treasures. Share these small surprises on Valentine's Day!

MATERIALS

- small matchboxes
- variety of red and pink patterned and plain paper
- scissors
- glue stick
- markers, stickers, glitter, and other materials for decorating
- ruler
- tiny treats and treasures

3

4

BEN

5

1. Open the matchbox and remove the matches.

2. Cut a long strip of paper the same width as the matchbox's length. Use a glue stick to cover the matchbox sleeve in glue.

3. Wrap the strip of paper around the matchbox sleeve and press it in place. Glue the end of the strip down.

4. Decorate the box with stickers, glitter, or paper hearts. Be creative!

5. Cut a thin strip of plain paper long enough to fit around the sleeve. It should be about 1 inch (2.5 cm) wide. Cover one side of the strip in glue. Then wrap it around the box sleeve and press it in place. Write your Valentine's name on the strip.

6. Repeat steps 1 through 5 to create more little boxes. Stuff each box with tiny treats and treasures for your Valentines!

ITSY-BITSY FIREWORK BURSTS

Celebrate Independence Day with a sparkling display of wee fireworks!

MATERIALS

- shiny tissue paper or wrapping paper in various colors
- scissors
- disposable plates
- thick craft wire
- thin craft wire
- air-dry clay
- all-purpose glue

1. Cut the shiny paper into tiny pieces over a paper plate. Keep colors separated on different plates, or combine all colors on one plate.

2. Cut three to five pieces of thick craft wire of various lengths. None should be longer than your hand.

3. Cut fifteen to twenty-five smaller pieces of thin craft wire. These can also be different lengths. Make some as long as your finger. Make others a bit longer or a bit shorter. Twist several pieces around the end of each long piece of wire. These will be firework bursts.

4. Form a small ball of air-dry clay a bit smaller than a golf ball. This will be your fireworks' base. Press the base on a table to give it a flat bottom. Then set it aside.

5. Squeeze glue onto a plate. Lay one firework burst in the glue. Remove it, and sprinkle bits of the shiny paper on the glue. When the burst is coated, stick the bottom end of the long wire into the rounded top of the base to dry. Repeat with all wires.

6. Let the glue and clay dry overnight. Wrap the clay base in a small square of the shiny paper, and tie it with wire. Your wee fireworks are ready for their show!

TINY THANKSGIVING TURKEY

Craft an itty-bitty Thanksgiving bird that is too cute to eat!

MATERIALS

- 2 small beads
- 1 larger wooden bead
- all-purpose glue
- brown pipe cleaner
- ruler
- scissors
- feathers
- tiny googly eyes
- yellow craft foam

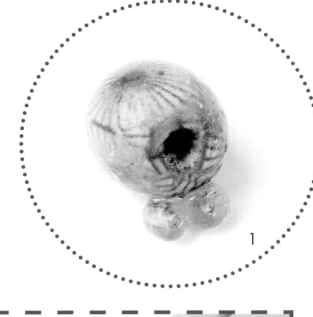

1

1. Glue the two small beads to the side of the wooden bead. Let the glue dry. These are the turkey's feet.

2. Cut a piece of pipe cleaner about 2 inches (5 cm) long. Thread it through the hole in the wooden bead.

3

3. Bend one end of the pipe cleaner to form the turkey's head. Bend the other end to look like the tail.

4. Cut small pieces off the feathers. Then glue the feather pieces to the tail end of the pipe cleaner. Let the glue dry.

5. Glue tiny googly eyes to the head end of the pipe cleaner.

6. Cut a tiny triangle out of yellow craft foam to make the turkey's beak. Glue it onto the head end of the pipe cleaner. Set your small gobbler out for Thanksgiving guests to enjoy!

4

PETITE PIÑATA

Celebrate Cinco de Mayo with teeny paper piñatas, ready to be popped!

MATERIALS

- card stock
- ruler
- pencil
- scissors
- tape
- colored tissue paper
- **confetti**
- string
- colored construction paper
- all-purpose glue

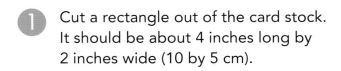

1

1. Cut a rectangle out of the card stock. It should be about 4 inches long by 2 inches wide (10 by 5 cm).

2. Make three folds in the card stock, each about 1 inch (2.5 cm) apart. Then fold the card stock to make a box, and tape it along the seam.

3. Cut two strips of tissue paper about 6 inches (15.2 cm) long. Each should be as wide as your card stock box.

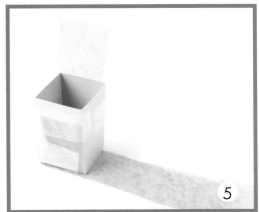

5

4. Tape the first piece of tissue paper to one of the box's edges. Stretch it over the box's opening. Tape the paper to the opposite edge, but don't cover the other box opening.

5. Now tape the second strip to another edge. Stretch the strip over the tissue-covered opening, and tape it to the opposite edge, leaving one end of the box open.

6

6. Fill the open end of the box with confetti.

Petite Piñata continued next page

Tiny Tip!

Make your own confetti by cutting tiny pieces out of tissue paper or construction paper.

Petite Piñata, continued

7. Stretch one tissue paper end to cover the open end of the box, and tape it in place. Make sure the paper is stretched tight (without ripping it). Repeat with the other tissue paper end.

9

8. Tape down any loose tissue paper edges.

9. Cut a piece of string about 6 inches (15.2 cm) long. Center the box on the string, then tie the string around the box. Tape the string in place. Then tie the two loose string ends together to make a loop.

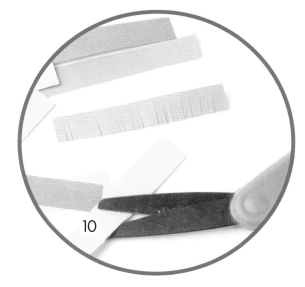

10

10. Cut many small strips of construction paper, each 2 to 3 inches (5 to 7.6 cm) long. Use a variety of colors. Cut notches in each strip to make fringe.

11. Glue the strips of fringe in rows around the box. Overlap the strips until the piñata is completely covered.

11

12. String up your super small piñata for Cinco de Mayo. Have friends and family take turns whacking it with a pencil until it bursts!

Show Your Holiday Spirit!

Finding fun ways to display your mini holiday crafts makes them seem even more adorable. Spread some candy beneath your petite piñata to show how small it really is. Drinking glasses look huge next to your tiny creation. Think of special ways to show off your other projects. Be creative, and have fun!

Wrapping Up
CLEANUP AND SAFEKEEPING

It's time to clean up! Make sure all pieces and tools are picked up. Store small parts in tins, containers, or plastic bags. Then find a safe place to keep your mini holiday crafts where they will be not lost or damaged. When it's time to put your crafts on display, make sure they are out of reach of pets and younger siblings. Now you're ready to celebrate big holidays in a wee way!

Keep Crafting!

Get inspired to make more mini holiday crafts! Look at a calendar. What holidays are coming up? Think of the usual gifts, symbols, and decorations associated with that holiday. How could you make tiny versions of them to celebrate? Think big and create small!

GLOSSARY

coils: series of loops

confetti: small bits of colored paper often thrown as part of a celebration

examine: to study something carefully

excess: extra or more than is needed

fascinate: to cause great interest in something

festive: cheerful or lively

garland: a wreath or string with materials, such as leaves or flowers, that can be used as decoration

kinara: a candelabra with seven candles used in celebrating Kwanzaa

petite: small or trim

sequins: small shiny pieces of metal or plastic used to decorate objects or clothing

trinkets: small ornaments or objects that are seen as having value

Further Information

Braun, Eric. *Plan a Holiday Party*. Minneapolis: Lerner Publications, 2015.
Learn how to throw a fun holiday party where you can display your mini creations!

McGuire, Margaret, and Alicia Kachmar, Katie Hatz, and Friends. *Microcrafts: Tiny Treasures to Make and Share*. Philadelphia: Quirk Books, 2011.
Learn how to make more mini creations with this fun book.

Reece, Linda. *Holiday Crafts: 50 Projects for Year-Round Family Fun*. New York: Skyhorse Publishing, 2015.
Discover even more festive crafts you can make to celebrate the holidays in style.

Winter Holiday Crafts for Kids
http://www.pbs.org/parents/fun-and-games/activities-and-crafts/winter-holiday-crafts-for-kids
This website has all kinds of crafts to add some fun to winter holidays.

INDEX